D0931315

The Library of
Writing Skills™

A Step-by-Step
Guide to
Issue-Based
Writing

Lauren Spencer

rosen
central™

The Rosen Publishing Group, Inc., New York

*For the writers whose eyes, ears, and minds are open
to helping us see the world in an honest way*

Published in 2005 by The Rosen Publishing Group, Inc.
29 East 21st Street, New York, NY 10010

First Edition

Library of Congress Cataloging-in-Publication Data

Spencer, Lauren.
  A step-by-step guide to issue-based writing / Lauren Spencer.—1st ed.
      p. cm. — (The library of writing skills)
Includes bibliographical references and index.
ISBN 1-4042-0214-5 (library binding)
ISBN 1-4042-5306-8 (pbk.)
6-pack ISBN 1-4042-5312-2
1. English language—Rhetoric. 2. Report writing.
I. Title. II. Series: Spencer, Lauren. Library of writing skills.
PE1408.S66459 2004
808'.042—dc22
                                                          2004008938

Manufactured in the United States of America

Table of Contents

Introduction

Issue-based writing is a way to keep track and make sense of events going on in the world. It takes a specific subject, whether it's one in the national spotlight or one in the writer's immediate surroundings, and explains that subject so that it can be better understood. The different techniques of issue-based writing can also be helpful for writing research papers and essays. By using the five *Ws*—who, what, where, when, and why—along with interview techniques and astute observations, your issue-based story will convey clear meaning and impact. Journalism, which is writing for media such as newspapers, magazines, and the Internet, uses an issue-based style.

Issue-based stories depend on a writer's own perception of a situation, while providing enough factual information for the reader to fully understand the facts. Issue-based pieces can be written in the form of hard-hitting news features, human-interest stories, and editorials, which express the writer's opinion.

In this book we will examine how issue-based writing can grow from the germ of an idea into a solidly researched story that will deliver interesting facts, quotes, and anecdotes. We will look at the importance of language and how words can go beyond just their meaning to create a feeling about a subject. We'll also investigate a variety of writing techniques to fully understand how issues in our world can come to life in many different ways. Along with the importance of finding an audience for issue-based writing, we will look at ways to grab a reader's attention in just the right manner.

Issue-based writing depends on the author seeing the world with fresh eyes and an open mind, ready to ask questions if necessary. The issues don't need to be earth shattering; they just need to move you in such a way that you'll want to know more.

Choosing Your Topic and Technique

Issue-based stories are always nonfiction, which means that they are based on facts. There are various ways that issue-based pieces can be written. They can be news stories that describe a real event, feature articles that transport the reader into the "shoes" of their subjects, or editorials that express the author's viewpoint. Issue-based writing can bring a reader to tears, laughter, or both at the same time. The style in which you choose to write your issue-based piece will depend upon the message and personality you'd like your story to convey. If your style has already been chosen for you in an assignment, there are still a variety of ways to bring the piece to life.

News Story

A news story takes an event and tells the reader exactly what happened in

KEY

✔ **Understand the various styles used for issue-based writing.**

✔ **Choose a topic.**

✔ **Ultimately, an issue-based story exists to share interesting and timely information with the reader.**

that moment. By focusing on the facts of the story, a news piece delivers a straightforward narrative that sticks to the event being covered without imparting the opinion of its author. Example:

Hartwood County school officials met last night to discuss plans to build a new gym for Kennelly Middle School. Every member of the school board was there, along with many parents and teachers. The meeting took place in Hartwood's Town Hall. The meeting became louder when the subject turned to using the existing staff parking lot for the gym. Many of the teachers and school officials felt that another area for parking should be mapped out so that they would not lose their parking spaces.

It was decided that construction on the new building will begin on April 12 and that a new parking area would be proposed to replace any space that is lost due to the new gym. The project would be finished by the start of the 2006 school year.

ASK YOURSELF

☐ Have I decided on a particular issue-based style?

☐ Is my topic focused?

Feature Article

A feature article explains an issue from the viewpoint of the main subject. This type of issue-based piece can include more emotional information than a news story because it often relies on the feelings of the subject and author to put the issue in context.

Example:

Mr. Rickburn sat tensely in Hartwood's Town Hall waiting for the school board meeting to begin. As people filed in, they did a double take because he looked very different. Usually, Mr. Rickburn, Kennelly's gym teacher, dresses in sweatpants and a sweatshirt. Wearing a suit, he gave off a very different impression.

Mr. Rickburn was at the meeting to present facts on why the new school gym will need to expand into space currently occupied by the staff parking lot. While he knew that this was not a popular opinion, Mr. Rickburn was able to prove why the gym needs to be larger. The Kennelly student body has increased 30 percent in the

last year, and Mr. Rickburn sees parents and kids
who come to basketball games and wrestling meets
standing in the gym since there's no room
anywhere for them to sit.

Editorial

An issue-based editorial is focused on the opinion of the writer and is therefore written in the first person. This type of piece reflects how the author feels about a topic in no uncertain terms. An important point to remember is that an issue-based editorial presents both sides of the issue, while imparting to the reader the reasons why the author feels his or her opinion is worthwhile. Example:

After attending the Hartwood Town Hall
meeting last night regarding the building of
the new Kennelly Middle School gymnasium,
I've come to the conclusion that this community
works best when it's under pressure. It is my
opinion, based on the large crowd that filled the
meeting hall, that even when we don't all agree,
we still pull together to get things done. It has
been obvious for a while that the school needs a
new gymnasium.

> As the school's gym teacher, Mr. Rickburn, pointed out at the beginning of the meeting, the student body has grown beyond the amount of space currently offered.
>
> I think we should consider expanding the entire school. It's wrong that students are forced to take classes in the gymnasium, as is currently happening. There just aren't enough classrooms. I know this feeling firsthand, because I'm one of those students who has to sit in the bleachers during health class. It is not a good way to learn. I feel that just as we pulled together last night and okayed the construction of a new gym, we should put our force into expanding the school itself.

Searching for a Topic

Now that you've decided on an issue-based style, you need a topic to write about. There are interesting topics all around you. Issue-based topics need to deal with a situation of interest to both you and your readers. Think of a subject that is timely and gripping. You may have already been assigned a topic to cover for an issue-based piece, but if not, look around you for ideas, or read the community section of your local newspaper.

There are a number of ways to gather and then narrow down your choices. Many writers carry around slender, pocket-sized "reporters" notebooks, but any blank paper will do as long as you keep it handy. Make a note when something catches your eye or ear. Ask yourself questions as you look around you. Is something happening in your community that may affect others? If so, how will it affect them and why?

A sure way to invite your readers to climb inside your issue-based story is to find something that they will feel strongly about. Look for things that are happening in your neighborhood. People love to relate to a situation where they know the location and the people involved. Or, if you're new to the area and you find an issue that relates somehow to where you've come from, that can also be interesting.

Issues that tug at the heart or involve drama or conflict make great topics for issue-based stories. Keep in mind that a certain amount of time may go by between when you decide on a topic and when you write the story, so make sure that the issue you cover is one that has "legs." This slang term that reporters sometimes use means a story has enough meaning to stand the test of time.

Look at the newspaper, watch the news, or go to an online news source and find a story. Examine it and then rewrite the story using each of the issue-based techniques:

- As a news story using just the facts
- As a feature story through the eyes of the main character
- As an opinion piece expressing how you feel about the story

2 Prewriting

As with any assignment, there will probably be a due date, meaning you have a deadline to finish the piece. Knowing what that deadline is will help you plan your time for the researching and writing of your story. With an issue-based topic, the investigation and research you do before you start your first draft is very important. It is the gathering of information that will fill out your news story, feature, or editorial so that the reader will feel that he or she is getting the most out of the topic.

There are many different resources available to help you gather the information you need. First of all, a curious mind is necessary. Take your topic and do some probing. If you are writing about something you've heard, let's say about art classes being cut from the school's curriculum, make a list of people you can talk to who will have information about this potential change. Interviewing, which is when you talk to people about a specific topic, is a great way to get firsthand facts about your subject. Before you approach the people whom you want to interview, come up with questions to ask them. Be prepared with a series of important points that you want to go over so that you get as much out of the moment as you can. Be relaxed and focused so that the interview will be more like a conversation ("Can I ask you some questions about . . . ?") rather than an interrogation ("Tell me all you know, now!").

Be Flexible

As you speak with people, be open to the fact that your idea may shift a little as you investigate it further. For instance, if you are pursuing a story on your school's decision to cut art classes, you may find out by talking to people that there is a new art studio opening next to the school that will hold after-school sessions. This may prove to be a more interesting viewpoint, so a slight shift in your focus would make the story better.

As you dive deeper into the topic, consider your angle. The angle of the story is the point of view that you, the author, bring to the piece. It is the foundation on which the story is built. Issue-based pieces depend on both a solid topic and a strong author's voice. Developing a solid angle will help keep you on track as you gather information.

A good way to keep your viewpoint focused and your information organized is with a graphic organizer called a gathering grid. This method of organizing is often combined with notes taken on index cards. This will help you keep track of your thoughts and your sources. Sources, which are places where you find information, can include books, the Internet, and people you interviewed for the story. Keep the gathering grid with you as you do further research. The index cards will work together with the grid to organize the information for your piece.

The Gathering Grid

At the top of a blank page, write your topic. Down the left-hand side of the sheet, write a list of questions using the basic five *W*s (who, what, where, when, why) in no particular order. In the columns, write the

TOPIC: New Art Studio

	Interviews (blue index cards)	Newspaper (yellow index cards)	Magazine (green index cards)	Internet (white index cards)
How will this replace school art classes?	Mr. Solly, vice principal (note 1)		*New York Times* article about other school budget cuts (note 1)	Local school board Web site (note 1)
What will the schedule be?	Ms. Burly, school principal (note 2)			
Who is making the decision so that this will happen?	Ms. Burly (note 3), Mr. Arlene, art teacher (note 4)	*The Eagle*, school newspaper (note 1)		

	Interviews (blue index cards)	Newspaper (yellow index cards)	Magazine (green index cards)	Internet (white index cards)
Who will attend these classes?	Mr. Arlene (note 5), Mr. Solly (note 6), mom (note 7)			Local school board Web site (note 2)
How do students feel about it?	Gary (note 8), Sam (note 9), Sally, Jen, Lyndsay at lunch table (note 10)		*New York Times* article about other school's students feelings (note 2)	Online chat with students at other schools (note 3)
Why is this happening?	Mr. Solly (note 11) Ms. Wyler, district leader (note 12)			
Where will students go instead of art class?	Ms. Burly (note 13), Mr. Arlene (note 14)	*The Eagle* (note 2) a school newspaper (note 3)		
When is this set to begin?	Ms. Burly (note 15)			

Example (Blue Index Card for Interviews):

1. Mr. Solly, Vice Principal: "This studio will replace the regular art classes in the school by having students attend after-school sessions next door. While the students won't be graded, they will be given extracurricular credit for attending."

location of where the information was found. Then, on the index cards, write what that information is. Color code your index cards for easy access.

Tips for Interviewing

- Find the right person for the topic—make sure that he/she is informed.
- Set up the interview by allowing enough time to talk without feeling rushed.
- Bring a pen, a pad of paper, and if you'd like, a small tape recorder. Always let your subject know that you are tape recording his or her comments.
- Do not ask questions that only require a "yes" or "no" answer. For example, if you ask, "Will this new art studio replace all of our school art classes?" the answer may be "yes" or "no." Ask the question in such a way that the subject has to give an explanation. "*How* will the new art studio replace our school art classes?" By starting your question with "how" (or, "who," "what," "when," "where," or "why") you will be guaranteed a more detailed answer.
- Have your questions written in the order you'd like them answered, but be flexible enough to allow more free-form follow-up questions.
- Listen carefully. This will lead to follow-up questions because he or she might say something that will lead to another interesting point.
- After you've asked all your questions, go over what you've written. Make sure you've got the person's name (and its correct spelling). If needed, obtain his or her job title. Also make sure that you haven't skipped over anything.
- Be sure to thank the person for his or her time.

Sources

While you are gathering your sources, you can see how important it is to be organized. The Internet and library are useful for gathering information for your grid. These resources offer a chance to look through articles in books, magazines, or newspapers. You can use a search engine and go to Web sites for research too. To search, type in your topic, for example, "Junior High art classes eliminated" and examine articles about the same issue in other schools.

Be very sure of the facts that you gather from all of your sources. If you are unsure about something, ask someone who can either confirm or deny the statement. Not everything we read online or in print is factual, so have a healthy amount of skepticism. This way you'll be sure that the story you write is not only factually correct, but also offers a balanced point of view.

ASK YOURSELF

- Do I have enough material to start my first draft?
- Have I backed up my information with facts and research?
- Is my research organized clearly so that I can easily find the information I need?
- Is my angle clear?

Writing Your First Draft

The details you have gathered will now become the material for your issue-based piece. Before you begin writing the story, make sure you have its nuts and bolts firmly planted in your head. These are the five *W*s that issue-based pieces revolve around.

To clear your vision and reestablish your angle or point of view, make a list of the basic five *W*s in your story (see example, page 19). Whether you are writing a news piece, feature article, or an editorial, you will need these basic, concrete facts before you begin.

Use this information to form your paragraphs while incorporating the details and quotes you've gathered during your research. Most issue-based stories are written in the form of an inverted triangle, meaning that the most important details are at the beginning of the piece and the least important are found at the end. The reason for this goes back to a time before computers, when newspaper

KEY

✔ **Organize the details.**

✔ **Begin writing.**

✔ **Use facts, anecdotes, and quoted material.**

```
Example:
Topic: Meghan White sent to the office for wearing a T-shirt
with a message on it
Who: Meghan White, seventh grader
What: Sent to the office
When: Last week
Where: First period homeroom, McKinnely Junior High
Why: Because her T-shirt had a written message on it
```

and magazine stories were cut with scissors to fit the space on the page. The story would be cut from the bottom to preserve the most important details, which came at the top.

The beginning of the piece contains its vital information. The story information then unfolds into supporting facts and anecdotes, which are brief stories that illustrate the topic or prove a point. In order to bring your reader into the core of your story, you'll want to develop a lead. This is something like a "Hey there" moment that creates interest in the story by immediately grabbing the reader's attention. Take your time developing your lead by looking over your notes for something that stands out. Example:

```
"Hold Me," read the glittery words on the
front of Meghan White's T-shirt. And at
that moment, Meghan truly did look as if
she needed to be held as she tried to
hold back her tears.
```

ASK YOURSELF

☐ Have I stayed on topic for my first draft?

☐ Does my lead sentence grab the reader's attention?

☐ Is the order of my story that of an inverted triangle?

☐ Are details, quotes, and anecdotes included?

By using something that puts the reader immediately into the moment, you've caught his or her attention and he or she will probably continue reading. From here, lay out the details and use your facts and anecdotes, along with quoted material, to bring the story to life. Each paragraph should add more information to support the subject. As you work your way further down the story, the information becomes less important. In your last paragraph, summarize and reiterate key points.

As you write your first draft, make sure that you have plenty of paper (or a blank computer screen) in front of you and enough time to complete the story without being rushed. You'll also want to have all of the research you've gathered around you. Your first draft is primarily meant to write all of your ideas without interruption. Do not worry about using correct spelling or grammar because those corrections will come during the editing of your piece. Even if you find places where you feel you need more information, don't let it stop you; just make yourself a note and keep writing. You can go back to add more data later. Example:

"Hold Me," read the glittery words on the front of seventh-grader Meghan White's T-shirt. And at that moment, Meghan truly did look as if she needed to be held as she tried to hold back her tears. Mr. Burrell, the homeroom teacher at McKinnely Junior High, had told her that her T-shirt went against school policy that states, "No student shall wear any piece of clothing bearing slogans."

It seemed as if many of her classmates were embarrassed for Meghan because no one looked her in the eye as she left the room. She was really freaked out by the reaction to her T-shirt.

Later that day, Meghan was seen wearing an oversized white T-shirt. In the lunchroom, Sarah Leiter, a fellow seventh grader, said, "I don't understand why the school makes such a big deal about words on T-shirts."

When asked that same question, Mr. Tetley, the counselor, commented, "The reason for this school rule is because words and phrases on T-shirts can often be very distracting. There can be inappropriate messages that embarrass or provoke people." He related an episode that happened three years ago when two eighth-graders got into an argument after one of them made a comment about the other's sports team T-shirt.

The school's dress code policy is taken very seriously at McKinnely, and this was proven again in the case of Meghan White.

Characteristics of Good Writing

All students must adhere to some basic rules if they want to sharpen their writing skills. Simply put, following these guidelines will help you shape poor or ineffective writing, or polish existing skills to make them more powerful.

CONCEPT: The main idea or topic of your written work is like a tree trunk. It contains all of the nutrients to fortify your story. Its main points are like branches that flow from the concept's base. Informative details can grow like budding leaves from those branches and can take the form of detailed descriptions, anecdotes, quoted or paraphrased information, statistics and other hard data, or just general facts.

ORDER: The way in which your tree—or concept—grows, or the way it is organized, is as equally important as your main idea. Without the proper organization, good ideas can't grow to reach their full potential. While there are many ways to organize your piece (chronologically, for instance, or by using the inverted triangle method), you must adhere to whatever design you have chosen. Having a good organizational strategy in place will help you make the transitions from point to point more easily.

STYLE: The style of a written work is sometimes referred to as the "author's voice." You impart this individual style to your writing. Your author's voice is like a personal signature that only you can give your work; it lets the reader know that you are giving something of yourself in your piece that is different from any other writing that he or she may read. Your unique author's voice should be evident from the first sentence, or lead, to the last sentence, or conclusion.

WORD CHOICE: Using precise words to convey specific meanings or emotion in your work is as important as your concept, order, and author's voice. Appropriate words can give your writing power like nothing else can. Always scan your draft to make sure that each word that you have chosen is the best word to express the full meaning of your concept or idea.

RHYTHM: The flow of sentences in your writing determines if the work has rhythm and momentum. As a rule, you want to vary your sentence length and structure throughout your written work. This means that you should have a mix of both short and long (compound and complex) sentences that propel your concept. Always read your work aloud to get a sense of its overall rhythm.

MECHANICS: The mechanical elements of your writing are the key points that determine if it is correct or not. These elements include the conventions of spelling, grammar, usage, punctuation, capitalization, and creating solid paragraphs (each with a main point). Always proofread and edit your work line by line while considering all of these conventions separately. Also, an excellent way to check the spelling of each word is to read the work backward from its end to its beginning

This news piece used all of the five *W*s in the first paragraph. If needed, the piece could be cut from the bottom, because all the "facts" of this particular story were covered in the first two paragraphs. The author also did research to find out the school's policy, while relating anecdotes about actual events surrounding the subject. Quoted material was used to support the general topic. Remember, any time you use a person's words, whether written in a book, taken from a Web site, or from an interview, you must put them in quotation marks. If you write those words as if they were your own, then you are plagiarizing someone else's work. Plagiarism is very serious. In order to avoid this, make sure that you keep track of where you've gotten your information. This way you can give credit where credit is due.

Revising Your First Draft

After you've finished the first draft of your issue-based piece, think about a title that will enhance your article. A title is very important for issue-based writing because it is the first thing to grab a reader's attention. Even before your lead draws a reader in, a title—called a headline in the world of journalism—will make someone want to know more. Think about a title that is concise and to the point. Focus on active verbs to get your view across. Don't use the same wording as your lead sentence.

For a news article, see how you can summarize the event without being obvious. For instance, if your piece is about the fact that your science class uses old textbooks, come up with something more appealing than "Old Textbooks Used in Science Class." Think about something specific to tie in the theme, like "Old Textbooks and New Students Make a Frustrating Mix." Wordplay on the subject can elicit a reader's attention.

KEY

- ✔ **Add a catchy or playful title.**

- ✔ **Revisit the piece to determine if more research is needed.**

- ✔ **Tighten up sentences, paragraphs, and transitions.**

Something along the lines of "Science Students Living in the Stone Age" may pique his or her curiosity.

Editorial pieces depend on your viewpoint to deliver the reader into the writing; therefore a title expressing your opinion would be best. Think about how you might announce your point of view out loud. Would that work for a title? "My Science Textbooks Are Driving Me Crazy" will give the reader direct insight into your feelings. With all issue-based titles, you want to leave just enough to the imagination so that the reader is curious enough to read on.

Revisit Your Story

Revision gives you the chance to look again at what you've written and make it even better. It's a sign that you think highly about your work and want to improve it. For the most productive view into what you've written, take a break from your story and let it "breathe." This will allow you to get a fresh perspective on the writing, as if you're seeing it again for the first time. Don't wait too long to get back to it, though. You don't want to lose interest and then let the piece go unfinished, since your excitement about the subject is what makes it fresh.

Once you pick it up again, grab a different colored pen or pencil, and read the piece aloud. You can do this just for yourself or in front of someone else. Mark any words that you stumble over or sentence sequences that are confusing. Then you can come back and make changes.

Note the additions or edits clearly on your page. Make sure that the meaning of your piece is as clear as it can be. Sometimes confusion happens when a sentence uses too many words. If you find that your sentences go on for too long, look for places where they can be simplified and broken up into more concise thoughts. Also make sure that each paragraph contains just one idea. As one thought comes to an end and another begins, start a new paragraph.

A good way to keep ideas and paragraphs on track is to understand and improve sentences. Sentences are the threads that weave the whole story together, and are crucial to the rhythm of your story. Working to improve their structure can only improve your writing.

Verbs

You want your verbs to agree with the rest of your sentences so everything can flow smoothly. Keep track of singular and plural subjects and how they

Sentence Structure

The basic parts of a sentence are the subject, which is the focus of what is being talked about, and the predicate, which says something about the subject. A simple predicate is a verb, while other descriptive words in the sentence add to, or modify, that verb. Example:

Our science textbooks (*subject*) are completely out of date (*predicate*).

In the previous sentence, the simple predicate is the verb "are," while "completely out of date" completes the predicate and the sentence.

go together with verbs. Also, examine tenses to make sure they are in agreement with each other. Example:

My science textbook is very old.

(Singular verb because the sentence deals with only one textbook.)

Our science textbooks are very old.

(Plural verb because there is more than one textbook being mentioned.)

My science textbook was first used in this school thirty years ago.

(The verb is in the past tense because the sentence deals with something that already happened.)

My science textbook is only useful for a few chapters.

(The verb is in the present tense because the sentence is pointing out something that is currently happening.)

My science class would be better if it could get some updated textbooks.

(The verb is in the future tense because the sentence is forecasting into the future.)

Types of Sentences

Sentences are meant to deliver all kinds of messages so the way you write them will add to their impact. There are choices in the types of sentences you can use to get your point across in an interesting way.

Simple Sentence

A simple sentence states only one complete thought using a subject and predicate. Example:

My science textbook is old.

Compound Sentence

A compound sentence joins two or more simple sentences with either punctuation or a coordinating conjunction. Coordinating conjunctions are joining words like "and," "or," "but," and "so." Examples:

My science textbook is old; it's very frustrating.

(A semicolon is used to join these two complete sentences.)

My science textbook is old so it's very frustrating.

(A coordinating conjunction is used to join the two complete sentences.)

Complex Sentence

When a sentence that contains a dependent clause, which can't stand alone because it's an incomplete thought, it's called a complex sentence. Example:

My science textbook, which is very out of date, makes me frustrated.

(The clause "which is very out of date" adds more detail.)

Declarative Sentence

This type of sentence makes a statement. Example:

My science textbook contains outdated information.

Interrogative Sentence

An interrogative sentence is a question.
Example:

Is a textbook considered outdated after twenty years?

Rhetorical Question

A rhetorical question is a question for which no response is expected. Example:

I ask you, is it right that our science class has to use outdated textbooks?

Imperative Sentence

An imperative sentence gives a command to the reader. Example:

Think about how frustrating it is to have an outdated textbook when you're trying to understand something as complicated as science.

Exclamatory Sentence

An exclamatory sentence relays a strong sense of emotion. Example:

It would be fantastic to have new twenty-first century science textbooks!

If you use a variety of sentence styles, your reader will get the most he or she can out of your story. Take time to examine all the sentences in your draft to determine if they should be more varied .

5 Editing Your First Draft

Before your issue-based story makes an appearance in the world, you'll want to make sure that the facts you've used are correct. In order to fact-check a story, you'll need to have your research and interviews handy for reference. Go over the proper names you've used to make sure they are spelled correctly. Make sure that every person's job title is correct. If you have any questions about these issues, double-check them in order to verify the information. Oftentimes, if the person works in an office, there will be someone there that can help you.

Any dates, whether they are of births, deaths, or national or local events, need to be checked for accuracy. Encyclopedias are a great source for general information, while a local city office will often have data to confirm events or dates in your immediate area. The Internet is also a great resource for fact-checking, since

KEY

✔ **Make sure facts and names are correct.**

✔ **Get a second opinion.**

✔ **Complete a spelling and grammar check.**

you can usually find encyclopedias, government information, and other material online.

Take your time when you are fact-checking your issue-based piece. Never be embarrassed to re-approach a person you've interviewed to make sure you've gotten his or her quotes and information correct. In the end, you'll want the person to be proud of the piece you've written.

Outside Opinions

Once you feel that all your thoughts and facts are in order, enlist outside help. This step will be really helpful in giving you the confidence to stand behind your work with pride. Choose someone who you know will spend time reading your article and who you can trust to give you an honest opinion of it. Friends or family members can be of help as long as you let them know that you need them to share their thoughts in a straightforward and constructive manner. Often people who are close to us feel that they might hurt our feelings with criticism, but constructive criticism is useful. This is when someone comments on how to make something better as opposed to just saying it isn't right. Keep in mind that this is only the opinion of your reader, but listen with an open mind if he or she has suggestions about how a sentence or thought could be clearer. With constructive criticism, there is no such thing as a put-down. Instead of "Your title is boring" you want to hear "Your title could be more exciting if . . . "

ASK YOURSELF

☐ Have I checked all name spellings and facts?

☐ Are constructive criticisms incorporated?

☐ Is the final spelling and grammar check complete?

You can also choose to use constructive criticism in a group setting by reading your issue-based article aloud. Have a question and answer session afterward. This is helpful to find out what part of the piece people responded to the most, which might give you ideas for moving certain ideas closer to the beginning or dropping certain facts altogether.

Final Check

Once you've made all your changes, it's time to do a final spelling and grammar check. If you've written your article on paper, then use a different colored pen to circle any questionable words and look them up in the dictionary. If your piece was written using a computer, then employ the spell-check function. Your computer will also probably have a grammar check function, but if it doesn't, or your piece is handwritten, then check your punctuation and grammar with a reference manual. Example:

Living with Disruption
Ever since fourth grade, there's been a student in my class who is loud and disruptive. I'm not going to name names, but it makes me angry that there hasn't been more done to try and help both him and the students who have to deal with his

actions. Whenever he isn't in school, the class breathes a sigh of relief. Even when the teacher sends him to the office, he's usually back by that same afternoon. Students are distracted from their work because they have to put up with his behavior on a daily basis.

According to a foundation called the National Center for Education Statistics, students aged twelve through eighteen were victims of about 1.9 million crimes in the year 2000. While the article also mentions that school violence has gone down since the 1990s, those numbers still seem high.

When asked about violent students at our school, Sherman Junior High, Mr. Dilly, the seventh-grade guidance counselor, commented, "When a troubled student does surface, the administration is very prepared to help that person in any way it can."

When I asked him why it seems so hard to keep disruptive kids out of the classroom, Mr. Dilly said, "It takes quite a lot for a student to be classified as disruptive. At that point we have to call the police, which is a last resort. We'd rather work out the problem at school."

While I think that's an admirable thing to do, I have a hard time accepting it when I'm sitting in class being distracted from my work. Fellow seventh-grader Sarah Morely agrees. She says she has never felt unsafe until she found herself in the same class as this student. It's not as if I want police patrolling the hallways, but I do want to learn what I need in order to go on to college.

New York City's mayor Michael Bloomberg said in a January 2004 article, "For too long, we've slowly found ourselves sinking further and further into a pit where anything is tolerated, where the teachers don't have a safe environment, where the teachers can't do their job and the students can't learn." While I don't think Sherman is that bad, I do agree that tolerating more and more at the expense of students' learning is wrong.

This editorial piece grabs the reader's attention with its title. It also uses all the five *W*s in the first paragraph. The author did research and interviewed a source for the piece. All of those items and quotes were fact-checked for name spellings and correctness. Notice that the source of Mayor Michael Bloomberg's comment was included and that his

Proofreading Guide

If you've given your article to a teacher, student, or adult to read it through, they may have used proofreading marks for corrections. Here is a guide to tell you what those symbols mean.

⌃	insert a comma	ℒ	delete	#	a space needed here
⌄	apostrophe or single quotation mark	∼	transpose elements	¶	begin new paragraph
∧	insert something	⌣	close up this space	NO ¶	no paragraph
＂ ＂	use double quotation marks	⊙ ⊗	use a period here		

statement was put in quotation marks. Also, note how the conclusion is cleary summarized in the article's final statement. Now, consider these points when reading your article or editorial.

6 Presentation

As you put your issue-based piece into its final form, think about how quickly most people respond to what something looks like. The presentation of your piece will make an important first impression on your reader. No matter what style of issue-based writing you have chosen, your final draft should be straightforward in type style and font size. Whether your story is handwritten or typed, it needs to be clear and legible, so that your audience is not distracted from its content. Finally, check that your name appears clearly on your article.

Once you've written the final draft of your story and included all your changes, there are elements that can be added to enhance the piece. Photos are a great way to illustrate an issue-based story. If you use a photo that you find online or through another form of media, check with your instructor about using it, as you might need to mention its original source. It's fun to use photos that you've taken yourself to add to your story.

KEY

✔ **Investigate different visual elements.**

✔ **Think of places to present and share your work.**

Authors who write editorial columns will often include pictures of themselves so that the reader can see whose opinion they are reading.

If you are writing your issue-based piece to be printed in a newspaper or magazine, you may be asked to format the story into columns. This is something that you can go over with whoever is in charge of the layout. A layout is the design and arrangement of a story before it is reproduced or printed.

Places to Present

You can share your issue-based piece in a variety of ways. If your school has a newspaper or magazine, approach its staff with your story. You can also volunteer to be assigned pieces through a school newspaper or magazine if you decide you'd like to be further involved in the world of journalism. Think about a local community paper or magazine that might enjoy publishing your take on an issue-based story. These types of publications usually focus on local events, so if your issue-based piece fits that category, send it in. (Remember to always check the submission guidelines first.)

There are also opportunities for publishing your piece in age-appropriate national magazines. Online, you can find a list of places to send your work. Always check with an adult before submitting stories online because it's important to have another set of eyes look over any rules and regulations that may apply to submitting work. Also, an adult can make sure

ASK YOURSELF

☐ Will the format of
the piece draw the
reader in?

☐ Are there places to
share this work?

☐ Are there other
issue-based styles
to explore?

that the site is reputable. These sources often have very specific requirements. Follow them closely, so that your writing ends up in the right hands. It may take a while before you hear a response but don't get frustrated, just be proud that you've gotten this far!

Photojournalism

People often say that a picture is worth a thousand words. This can be very true in storytelling. Photojournalism is a way to tell an issue-based story using the power of visuals to get a point across. While text is an important element in a photojournalistic story, the main focus is on the photograph and how it relays to the viewer what is going on. A photojournalistic story can be made up of one or more photos, but just enough to cover the main point of the issue. For instance, a series of pictures featuring the homecoming of soldiers can deliver a greater emotional story regarding the issues of war through the looks on the soldiers' faces. While captions below the photos are necessary to explain what is being viewed, the eye is more directly drawn to the visual angle.

You can create your own photojournalistic story too. Take a camera (any type will do, from digital to disposable) and walk around your school or neighborhood and snap away. Once you see your pictures, pick out the ones that deliver the greatest force. You may only find one. Then write a caption underneath explaining the who, what, where, when, and why of

Journalistic Terms

There are very specific terms that are used with journalistic work for newspapers, magazines, or online sources. Here are some of them:

Byline: The writer's name.

Dateline: A dateline is written at the beginning of the story that gives the place and date of the event. Used most often for daily newspaper stories. Example:

Florida, Jan. 9 – Disney World announced today the addition of a new speedy roller coaster.

Deadline: The date or time that a story must be finished.

Headline: The title of a newspaper story or article.

Layout: The arrangement on a page of stories, articles, and artwork before it goes to print.

Photo caption: The lines underneath a photograph that explain who is in the picture and/or what is going on.

Photojournalism: A form of journalism in which a photo, or series of photos, is used to tell the story. These are usually accompanied by detailed captions.

Subhead: An explanation under the headline that further explains the story. Example:

Headline: Disney World Introduces a New Roller Coaster
Subhead: Officials Say It Will Be the Fastest in the World

Text: The main body of printed or written matter on a page.

the picture. Be sure to get permission from the subject of your photo before you take it and let him or her know if you're going to have it printed in a newspaper or magazine.

Editorial Cartoons

If you enjoy drawing or cartooning, another way to express yourself in an issue-based style is through editorial cartoons. You can often find them on the editorial pages of newspapers. They differ from the cartoons you find on the funny pages of newspapers or in comic books because they are meant to make a statement. They deal with timely issues and use humorous or witty visuals and text to deliver a pointed message regarding the topic.

You can try it for yourself by choosing one from the newspaper, whiting out the words, then filling in the text yourself, based on what you see

Thanks to new security precautions,
Bob's surprise party held no surprises.

Editorial cartoons often examine serious issues and present them in a satirical way, as cartoonist Mike Baldwin did in this recent illustration. While some have touted the guidelines defined in the USA PATRIOT Acts I and II as necessary safety precautions, others have criticized them as being too overreaching. Still others believe that the new laws violate precious civil liberties.

depicted and what message you think the artist wants to get across. Or, if you enjoy drawing, sketch out a timely issue of your own and add your own text.

Hopefully this book has covered enough of the basics in order to get your issue-based writing going in a positive and forceful direction. If journalism piques your interest, try taking specific journalism classes if they are offered at your school. If not, try working as a writer or editor for your school newspaper. You can also read books or Web sites related to issue-based writing to sharpen your skills. Try the following Web sites for more information: the Journalist's Primer, an online guide to journalism style and grammar (http://www.papertrained.org/primer.html); reporter.org, resources for reporters (http://www.reporter.org/beat); and a searchable database of media sites, resources, and articles at the American Journalism Review (http://www.ajr.org/archive.asp).

Glossary

anecdote A short, entertaining account of an event.

angle The viewpoint of the piece.

article A complete piece of writing as in a newspaper or magazine.

assignment A task or mission.

chronological In the order that events happened.

complex sentence A sentence formed by one independent clause and one or more dependent clauses.

compound sentence A sentence in which two independent clauses are joined together with a coordinate conjunction.

conjunction A word used to connect individual words or groups of words.

constructive criticism Helpful remarks about shared writing.

content The substance of a piece, what is contained in a body of writing.

deadline The date or time by which something has to be completed.

declarative sentence A sentence that makes a strong statement.

dependent clause A clause that cannot stand on its own and depends on the rest of a sentence to make sense.

essay A piece of writing where a single topic is presented, explained, and described in an interesting way.

first draft The first writing of a piece without worrying about mistakes.

format The style or manner of a piece of writing.

heading Words located at the top of the page that include pertinent information about time, place, and author.

imperative sentence A sentence that gives a command to the reader.

independent clause A statement that expresses a complete thought and can stand alone as a sentence.

interrogative sentence A sentence in the form of a question.

journalism The collection and editing of news for presentation through the media.

nonfiction Stories that are true.

paragraph A passage of writing of one or more sentences that deals with a single topic.

phrase A group of related words that do not express complete thoughts.

plagiarism The taking of ideas, writing, etc., from another and passing them off as one's own.

proofreading Checking the final copy for any errors.

reporter A person who gathers and reports news.

revise To go back and survey.

rhetorical question A question for which no response or answer is expected.

source A person or place where information comes from.

subject The topic of a writing piece.

title The heading of a piece of writing.

topic The subject of a piece of writing.

transition A word or phrase that smoothly ties two ideas together .

verb A word that shows action.

For More Information

National Council of Teachers
   of English (NCTE)
Achievement Awards in Writing
1111 Kenyon Road
Urbana, IL 61801-1096
Web site: http://www.ncte.org

Reading, Writing, and Art Awards
Weekly Reader Corporation
200 First Stamford Place
P.O. Box 120023
Stamford, CT 06912-0023
Web site: http://
   www.weeklyreader.com

The Scholastic Art and Writing Awards
557 Broadway
New York, NY 10012
Web site: http://www.scholastic.com

Web Sites

Due to the changing nature of Internet links, the Rosen Publishing Group, Inc., has developed an online list of Web sites related to the subject of this book. This site is updated regularly. Please use this link to access the list:

www.rosenlinks.com/lws/isba

Getting Published

Merlyn's Pen
Fiction, Essays, and Poems by
America's Teens
P.O. Box 2550
Providence, RI 02906-0964
e-mail: Merlyn@MerlynsPen.com
Web site: http://www.merlynspen.com

Skipping Stones
A Multicultural Children's Magazine
P.O. Box 3939
Eugene, OR 97403-
e-mail: skipping@efn.org
Web site: http://
www.skippingstones.org

Stone Soup
The Magazine by Young Writers
and Artists
P.O. Box 83
Santa Cruz, CA 95063
Web site: http://www.stonesoup.com

TeenInk
P.O. Box 30
Newton, MA 02461
e-mail: submit@teenink.com
Web site: http://www.teenink.com

Teen Voices
P.O. Box 120-027
Boston, MA 02112-0027
e-mail: womenexp@teenvoices.com
Web site: http://www.teenvoices.com

Young Voices Magazine
P.O. Box 2321
Olympia, WA 98507
e-mail: support@
youngvoicesmagazine.com
Web site: http://
www.youngvoicesmagazine.com/

For Further Reading

Culham, Ruth. *6+1 Traits of Writing:
The Complete Guide.* New York:
Scholastic, 2003.

Fletcher, Ralph. *A Writer's Notebook:*

Unlocking the Writer Within You. New
York: HarperTrophy, 2003.

Sebranek, Patrick. *Writers Inc.: A Student
Handbook for Writing and Learning.*

Wilmington, MA: Great Source Educational Group, Inc., 2000.

Zaragoza, Nina. *Rethinking Language Arts: Passion and Practice* (Teaching and Thinking). New York: Routledge, 2002.

Bibliography

Ace Writing. "The Writing Process." 2002. Retrieved July 7, 2003 (http://www.geocities.com/ fifth_grade_tpes/index.html).

Creative Writing for Teens. "How to Format a Manuscript for Publication." 2003. Retrieved June 20, 2003 (http:// www. teenwriting.about.com/cs/ formatting/ht/FormatManu.htm).

Creative Writing for Teens. "Tips on Writing from the Creative Writing for Teens Community." 2003. Retrieved August 26, 2003 (http:// www.teenwriting.about.com/library/ submissions/bltipssub.htm).

English Biz. "Writing to Describe and Original Writing." 2003. Retrieved October 16, 2003 (http:// www.englishbiz.co.uk/mainguides/ describe.htm).

Feder, Barnaby J., "With the Apples Arriving by E-Mail, Teachers Adapt." *New York Times*, August 14, 2003, p. G5.

Guernsey, Lisa. "A Young Writer's Roundtable, via the Web." *New York Times*, August 14, 2003, p. G1.

Guide to Grammar and Writing. "Guide to Grammar and Writing." 2003. Retrieved August 1, 2003 (http://webster.commnet.edu/ grammar/index.htm).

Hewitt, John. "Fifteen Craft Exercises for Writers." Writers Resource Center Online. Retrieved June 25, 2003 (http://www.poewar.com/ articles/15_exercises.htm).

Kemper, Dave; Patrick Sebranek; Verne Meyer. *All Write: A Student Handbook for Writing & Learning*. Wilmington, MA: Great Source Education Group, 1998.

LEO: Literacy Education Online. "The Write Place Catalogue." 1997. Retrieved July 10, 2003 (http://leo.stcloudstate.edu/ acadwrite/descriptive.html).

Scholastic for Teachers. "Writing With Writers." 2003. Retrieved June 20, 2003 (http://teacher.scholastic.com/writewit/).

Stone Soup. "Links for Young Writers." 2004. Retrieved June 20, 2003 (http://www.stonesoup.com/main2/links.html).

Teacher Created Materials. "Language Arts." 2000. Retrieved July 21, 2003 (http://www.teachercreated.com).

Winthrop, Elizabeth. "Some Practical Advice on Writing and Publishing for Young Writers." 1998. Retrieved August 26, 2003 (http://www.elizabethwinthrop.com/advice.html)

Index

About the Author

Lauren Spencer is originally from California and now lives in New York City, where she teaches writing workshops in the public schools. She also writes lifestyle and music articles for magazines.

Photo Credit

P. 40 © Mike Baldwin/CartoonStock.com

Credits

Designer: Geri Fletcher; **Editor:** Joann Jovinelly